Athens

by Betsy Rathburn
Illustrated by Diego Vaisberg

BLASTOFF!
MISSIONS

BELLWETHER MEDIA
MINNEAPOLIS, MN

Blastoff! Missions takes you on a learning adventure! Colorful illustrations and exciting narratives highlight cool facts about our world and beyond. Read the mission goals and follow the narrative to gain knowledge, build reading skills, and have fun!

Traditional Nonfiction

Narrative Nonfiction

Blastoff! Universe

MISSION GOALS

> FIND YOUR SIGHT WORDS IN THE BOOK.

> LEARN ABOUT DIFFERENT TIMES IN ATHENS'S HISTORY.

> LEARN ABOUT DIFFERENT GROUPS WHO RULED ATHENS.

This edition first published in 2024 by Bellwether Media, Inc.

No part of this publication may be reproduced in whole or in part without written permission of the publisher. For information regarding permission, write to Bellwether Media, Inc., Attention: Permissions Department, 6012 Blue Circle Drive, Minnetonka, MN 55343.

Library of Congress Cataloging-in-Publication Data

Names: Rathburn, Betsy, author. | Vaisberg, Diego, illustrator.
Title: Athens / by Betsy Rathburn ; illustrated by Diego Vaisberg.
Description: Minneapolis, MN : Bellwether Media, 2024. | Series: Blastoff! Missions: Cities Through Time |
   Includes bibliographical references and index. | Audience: Ages 5-8 | Audience: Grades 2-3 | Summary:
   "Vibrant illustrations accompany information about the history of Athens. The narrative nonfiction text is intended
   for students in kindergarten through third grade."-- Provided by publisher.
Identifiers: LCCN 2023044969 (print) | LCCN 2023044970 (ebook) | ISBN 9798886877540 (library binding)
   | ISBN 9798886879421 (paperback) | ISBN 9798886878486 (ebook)
Subjects: LCSH: Athens (Greece)--History--Juvenile literature.
Classification: LCC DF285 .R38 2023 (print) | LCC DF285 (ebook) | DDC 938.5--dc23/eng/20230922
LC record available at https://lccn.loc.gov/2023044969
LC ebook record available at https://lccn.loc.gov/2023044970

Text copyright © 2024 by Bellwether Media, Inc. BLASTOFF! MISSIONS and associated logos are trademarks and/or registered trademarks of Bellwether Media, Inc.

Editor: Christina Leaf   Designer: Andrea Schneider

Printed in the United States of America, North Mankato, MN.

This is **Blastoff Jimmy**! He is here to help you on your mission and share fun facts along the way!

Table of Contents

Welcome to Athens!

Look around! We are in Athens, Greece. This city has an **ancient** past. It stretches back thousands of years. Let's explore it!

A Powerful Place

around 500 BCE

Listen up! The **assembly** is about to vote. People will decide on a new law. The Athens **city-state** is a powerful **democracy**!

assembly

Naí!

JIMMY SAYS

One assembly had as many as 6,000 people!

The Parthenon is finally finished. This **temple** honors the goddess Athena.

Parthenon

▶ **JIMMY SAYS** ◀

The temple held many statues. One was of Athena. It stood around 39 feet (12 meters) tall!

Below, people gather in a theater.
Plays are now popular!

404 BCE

The people no longer rule in Athens. They lost a war to Sparta.

They are forced to pull down the city's walls. The **golden age** of Athens is over.

Athens is part of the **Eastern Roman Empire**. The city has been forgotten for years. But it is growing again.

Christianity is growing, too. Those workers are building a new church!

12

The Parthenon has been hit!
Will it remain standing?

1834

Greece is finally free! Athens is its new capital. The city is an important center again.

King Otto

Athens only has 7,000 people.
But King Otto plans to grow it.
It will become a large city!

2004

The **Olympic Games** have come back to Athens! A new airport welcomes visitors. New subway trains zip people to the Games. Greek athletes will win 16 medals!

JIMMY SAYS

The Olympics began in Greece around 776 BCE. The first modern Games were held in Athens in 1896!

athletes

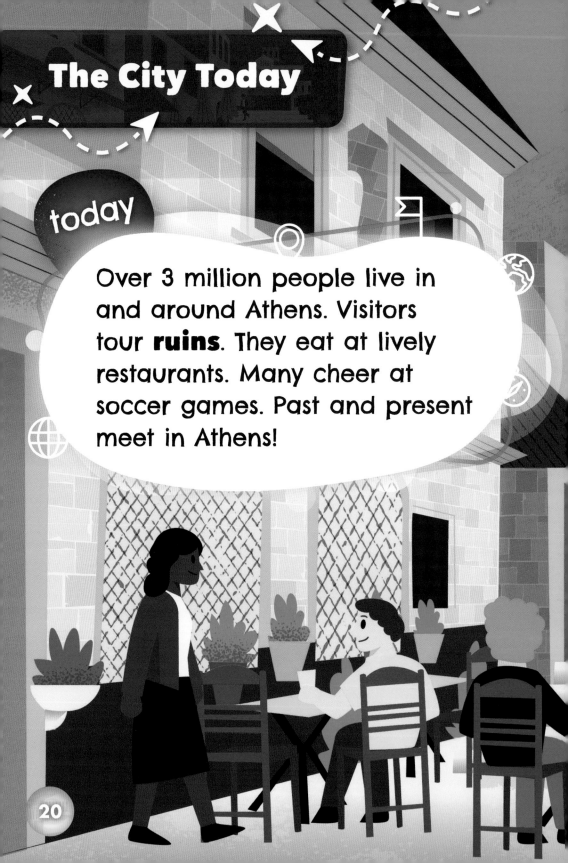

today

Over 3 million people live in and around Athens. Visitors tour **ruins**. They eat at lively restaurants. Many cheer at soccer games. Past and present meet in Athens!

Athens Timeline

around 500 BCE: Athens is one of the first democracies in the world

432 BCE: The Parthenon is finished

404 BCE: Athens falls to Sparta at the end of the Peloponnesian War

1000s CE: Christianity grows in Athens under the Eastern Roman Empire

1687: An attack on Athens damages the Parthenon

1834: Athens becomes the capital of the Kingdom of Greece

2004: Athens hosts the Olympic Games

Athens, Greece

Glossary

ancient—from long ago

assembly—a gathering of citizens for a vote

Christianity—a religion that follows the teachings of Jesus Christ and the Christian Bible

city-state—a city that governs itself

democracy—a system of government that allows people to vote on how the government is run

Eastern Roman Empire—parts of Europe, Asia, and North Africa under the control of one leader that began around 330 CE and lasted until 1453; the Eastern Roman Empire was also called the Byzantine Empire.

golden age—a period of great wealth and happiness

Olympic Games—worldwide summer or winter sports contests held in a different country every four years

Ottomans—members of the Ottoman Empire; the Ottoman Empire was a large empire that controlled parts of Europe, Asia, and North Africa.

ruins—the remains of something that was destroyed

temple—a building used for worship

To Learn More

AT THE LIBRARY

Davies, Monika. *Greece*. Minneapolis, Minn.: Bellwether Media, 2024.

Jones, Rob Lloyd. *See Inside Ancient Greece*. London, U.K.: Usborne, 2019.

Núñez, Jhonny. *The Ancient Olympic Games*. London, U.K.: Wayland, 2021.

ON THE WEB

FACTSURFER

Factsurfer.com gives you a safe, fun way to find more information.

1. Go to www.factsurfer.com.

2. Enter "Athens" into the search box and click 🔍.

3. Select your book cover to see a list of related content.

BEYOND THE MISSION

> WHAT FACT FROM THE BOOK DID YOU THINK WAS THE MOST INTERESTING?

> WHAT ARE SOME WAYS THAT ATHENS AFFECTED THE WORLD?

> WHAT SPORT WOULD YOU DO IF YOU WERE IN THE OLYMPICS? WHY?

Index